Playtime

Twist around,
Turn around,
Twirl around, and then
Swish about
And spin about,
And do it all again!

Twist around,
Whirl around,
As you have done before;
Spin about
And turn about,
And do it all once more!

Watch the spins,
Watch the turns,
Watch the twists and twirls,
In and out
And roundabout,
For busy boys and girls.

Unknown

Little People™ Big Book

About PLAYTIME

TIME LIFE for Children™

ALEXANDRIA, VIRGINIA

Table of Contents

One Is Fun

All Together Now

Play Ball!

One is Fun

Hide and Seek

When I am alone, and quite alone,
I play a game, and it's all my own.

I hide myself
Behind myself,
And then I try
To find myself.

I hide in the closet,
Where no one can see;
Then I start looking
Around for me.

I hide myself
And look for myself;
There once was a shadow
I took for myself.

I hide in a corner;
I hide in the bed;
And when I come near me
I pull in my head!

A.B. Shiffrin

5

The Velveteen Rabbit

A Retelling of the Story
by Margery Williams

Once upon a time, there was a lovely toy Velveteen Rabbit. He had pink silk ears, a tiny red thread nose, long whiskers, and a soft brown-and-white fuzzy coat. He was plump and soft, and just right for hugging.

When the Boy first saw him, he hugged the little Rabbit tightly and played with him for hours. But soon it was dinnertime, and the Boy forgot all about the Velveteen Rabbit. After that, the Rabbit was placed in the toy cupboard with all of the other toys.

The poor little Rabbit was lonely and uncomfortable in the cupboard. Most of the other toys were more expensive, and the mechanical toys said that they were real, so they rarely spoke to the Velveteen Rabbit. His only friend was the old Skin Horse.

One day the Velveteen Rabbit asked his friend, "What's REAL?"

"It's something that happens to you when you're loved," explained the Skin Horse. "It has nothing to do with being mechanical, like the toy trains." For a long time after that, the Velveteen Rabbit wondered how it would feel to be real. He wondered if it would ever happen to him.

One night the Boy couldn't find the china dog that always slept with him. So Nana reached into the toy cupboard and scooped up the Velveteen Rabbit.

"Here," she said to the Boy, "take your rabbit! He'll sleep with you." Then she tucked the little Rabbit into the waiting arms of the Boy.

That night, and for many more nights after, the Velveteen Rabbit slept with the Boy. Sometimes the Boy would talk to him or play games with him. But mostly the Boy snuggled up close to the little Rabbit and held him all night long. This made the Rabbit very happy.

Soon everywhere the Boy went, the Rabbit went too. They would go for rides in the park, picnic on the beach, or swing on the backyard swings. Once the Boy forgot the Rabbit in the garden, and Nana had to go looking for him with a flashlight.

"Please find my bunny," said the Boy, almost in tears.

"Stop crying," said Nana, once she found the Rabbit. "It's only a toy."

"No, it's not!" said the Boy, hugging the Rabbit tightly. "You mustn't say that. HE'S REAL!"

When the little Rabbit heard the Boy, he was so happy that his sawdust heart almost burst. He was no longer just a toy rabbit. He was REAL.

That summer, the Boy and the Velveteen Rabbit had a wonderful time. One evening, when the Velveteen Rabbit was sitting in the garden watching the ants play, he saw two very strange creatures. They were real rabbits. They looked just like him but they were somehow different.

One rabbit padded close to the Velveteen Rabbit and wiggled his nose at him. The two stared at each other.

"Come and play with us," said the rabbit, standing on his hind legs.

"I don't want to," said the Velveteen Rabbit, a little worried. "The Boy will be here soon. We have to be home before dark."

"We don't think you can play," said the other rabbits. "You don't smell like a real rabbit. You're just a toy."

"You're wrong! I'm a REAL rabbit," cried the Velveteen Rabbit. "The Boy said so."

But just then the Boy appeared and the two rabbits ran off into the woods.

Near the end of summer the Boy became ill. The doctor came to the house and said the Boy would get well. But all his old toys and books would have to be thrown away; the Boy could now play only with clean toys. The little Rabbit was tossed in an old sack with the rest of the Boy's toys and left outside with the trash.

That evening, the Rabbit peeped out of the sack and looked around the garden. He remembered all the wonderful times he and the Boy had together, and how he loved the Boy and now would never see him again. A sadness came over the little Rabbit and a tear, a real tear, trickled down his face and fell to the ground.

Then a wonderful thing happened. Where the tear fell, a beautiful flower grew. It had long emerald-green leaves surrounding a golden blossom. The Rabbit stared in amazement. Suddenly the petals of the flower opened and out stepped a fairy.

The fairy smiled at the Rabbit and gathered him in her arms. "Little Rabbit," she said sweetly, "I am the nursery magic fairy. I have come to make you a real rabbit."

"But I am real," said the Velveteen Rabbit.

"You were real to the Boy, who loved you," she said, "but soon you will be real to everyone."

With that, the fairy kissed the Rabbit, picked him up, and flew with him into the woods. When they reached a clearing, she put him down where some other rabbits were playing.

"Run and play, little Rabbit," she said. The little Rabbit sat silent and still. He didn't know that her kiss had made him real. Suddenly his nose itched. Without thinking, he lifted his front paw and scratched. Soon he was wiggling his ears and twitching his whiskers. He was real at last!

Before long, winter arrived, then spring, and finally summer. One warm day, the Boy was playing in the woods when he spotted a little rabbit with pink ears and brown-and-white fur. The Boy sat and looked at the rabbit, then smiled. Sure enough, it was the Velveteen Rabbit, who had come back to see the Boy he loved so much.

The Rainy-Day Playtime List

by Wendy Wax

*There are lots of rainy-day playtime ideas in this poem. Once you've read
and tried them, you can change some of them slightly and do them again!*

On Saturday morning, Scott awoke
To a dark, gray, gloomy sky,
No playground, no tag, no riding bikes—
He thought with a miserable sigh.

"Come downstairs," he heard Mom call.
"I've made a surprise for you!"
Scott rushed to the kitchen and happily found
A whole list of fun things to do:

"Set out on a terrific treasure hunt
For things that start with **T**:
Tulip, tiger, telephone,
Toy train, or a cup of tea!

12

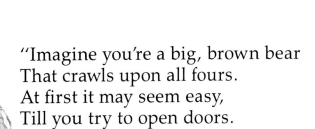

"Pretend the day is Backwards Day,
When good-byes mean hellos.
Wear all your clothing inside out.
Try writing with your toes!

"Imagine you're a big, brown bear
That crawls upon all fours.
At first it may seem easy,
Till you try to open doors.

"Sit upon your favorite rug
And say some magic words.
Imagine that you're soaring
Even higher than the birds.

"Try your hand at arts and crafts
With paper, paint, and glue
Crayons, scissors, cardboard, string—
All odds and ends will do.

13

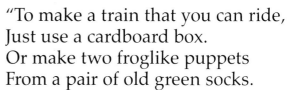

"To make a train that you can ride,
Just use a cardboard box.
Or make two froglike puppets
From a pair of old green socks.

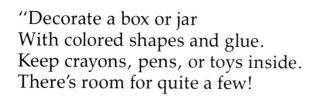

"Decorate a box or jar
With colored shapes and glue.
Keep crayons, pens, or toys inside.
There's room for quite a few!

"Make a card for a special friend
With fingerprint designs.
All you need is fingerpaint
And a felt-tip pen for lines.

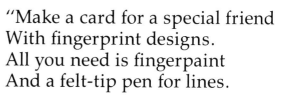

"Paint with pudding on a paper plate.
Make a necklace out of noodles.
Use your brightest, best crayons
To draw some silly doodles.

"If your stomach starts to growl,
It's probably time for lunch.
Now's the time to become a chef—
To make a snack to munch.

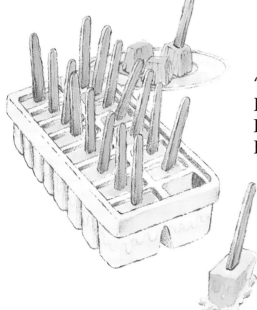

"Put an ice-cream stick in a pineapple chunk,
Put the chunk in an ice cube tray,
Fill the tray with juice and freeze it all—
It tastes just great that way!

"Guess how many cookies
Are jammed inside a jar.
Take off the lid and count them up
To see how close you are.

"Guessing games are lots of fun—
There are many different styles.
How many sections in an orange?
How many bathroom tiles?

"If you're feeling restless,
The mirror's the place to be.
Make lots of funny faces,
And you'll laugh hysterically!

"Make a list of the sounds you hear
From near or far away:
The buzz of the vacuum, the rain on the roof,
The noises of the day.

"Choose five words that start with **S**,
And put them all together
Now say your tongue twister five times fast—
You'll forget about the weather.

16

"Pretend you're in an orchestra.
Your tongue can make loud clicks.
And once you've got the rhythm,
Use your shoes for two drumsticks.

"Take your mind out for a 'walk':
Imagine you're on a trip.
Where will you stay? Who will you see?
Will you go by train or ship?

"Or you may choose to do nothing at all
But gaze at the window pane.
Just curl right up in a cozy chair
And listen to the rain."

CLASSIC FINGERPLAYS

The next time you are sitting indoors with nothing to do, try one of these fingerplays. They're sure to liven up your day, rain or shine!

Hickory, Dickory, Dock

Hickory, dickory, dock,
The mouse ran up the clock,
The clock struck one,
The mouse ran down,
Hickory, dickory, dock.

Hickory, dickory, dock...
***(Bend arm at elbow,
hold up, swing arm side to side)***

The mouse ran up the clock...
(Run fingers up arm)

The clock struck one...
(Hold up one finger)

The mouse ran down...
(Run fingers down arm)

Hickory, dickory, dock...
***(Bend arm at elbow,
hold up, swing arm side to side)***

The Eensy, Weensy Spider

The eensy, weensy spider
Ran up the waterspout.
Down came the rain
And washed the spider out.
Out came the sun
And dried up all the rain.
So the eensy, weensy spider
Ran up the spout again.

The eensy, weensy spider...
(Opposite thumb and forefingers climb up each other)

Down came the rain...
(Hands sweep down and open wide)

Out came the sun...
(Form circle over head with arms)

So the eensy, weensy spider...
(Opposite thumb and forefingers climb up each other again)

19

There Was a Little Turtle

There was a little turtle,
He lived in a box.
He swam in a puddle,
He climbed on the rocks.
He snapped at a mosquito,
He snapped at a flea,
He snapped at a minnow,
He snapped at me.
He caught the mosquito,
He caught the flea,
He caught the minnow,
But he didn't catch me!

There was a little turtle...
(Make small circle with hands)

He lived in a box...
(Make box with both hands)

He swam in a puddle...
(Wiggle one hand)

He climbed on the rocks...
*(Make a fist with the other hand.
Climb fingers of first hand
over fist)*

20

He snapped at a mosquito...
(Clap hands once each time turtle snaps at an animal)

He snapped at me...
(Point to self)

He caught the mosquito...
(Start with palm open, then move hand through air and quickly close fingers as if catching something, each time turtle catches an animal)

But he didn't catch me!
(Shake head no and point to self)

Grandma's Spectacles

Here are Grandma's spectacles
And here is Grandma's hat;
And here's the way she folds her hands
And puts them in her lap.

Here are Grandpa's spectacles
And here is Grandpa's hat;
And here's the way he folds his arms
And sits like that.

Here are Grandma's
spectacles...
*(Make circles with thumbs and
forefingers and place them over
eyes like glasses)*

And here is Grandma's hat...
*(Make triangle with both hands
and put on top of head)*

And here's the way she folds her
hands...
(Fold hands and place in lap)

22

Here are Grandpa's
spectacles...
*(Make bigger circles with fingers
and place over eyes like glasses)*

And here is Grandpa's hat...
*(Make a bigger triangle with
hands and place on head)*

And here's the way he folds his
arms...
(Fold arms with vigor)

And sits like that...
(Sit down with arms folded)

All Together Now

We're Racing,
Racing down the Walk

We're racing, racing down the walk,
Over the pavement and round the block.
We rumble along till the sidewalk ends—
Felicia and I and half our friends.
Our hair flies backward. It's whish and whirr!
She roars at me and I shout at her
As past the porches and garden gates
We rattle and rock
On our roller skates.

Phyllis McGinley

25

CLAPPING RHYMES

These are clapping games for two people. On the first word of each line ("Miss" in "Miss Mary Mack," for example), cross your arms against your chest. On the second syllable ("Mar-"), pat your thighs with your hands. On the third syllable ("-y"), clap your hands together. Then, for the rest of the line ("Mack, Mack, Mack"), clap your right hand against the other player's right, clap your own hands together, and then clap your left hand against the other player's left. Repeat for each line.

Miss Mary Mack

Miss Mary Mack, Mack, Mack,
All dressed in black, black, black,
With silver buttons, buttons, buttons
All down her back, back, back.

She asked her mother, mother, mother
For fifteen cents, cents, cents
To see the elephant, elephant, elephant
Jump over the fence, fence, fence.

It jumped so high, high, high
It reached the sky, sky, sky
And never came back, back, back
Til the Fourth of July, July, July.

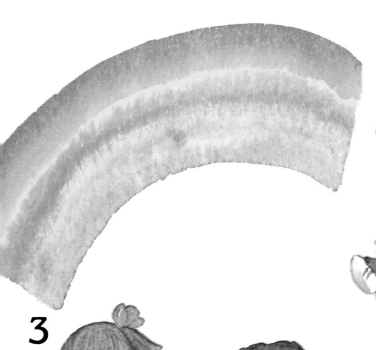

Oh, Little Playmate

3

Oh, little playmate,
Come out and play with me.
And bring your dollies three.
Climb up my apple tree.
Slide down my rainbow,
Into my cellar door,
And we'll be jolly friends
Forevermore, more, more.

Oh, little playmate,
I cannot play with you.
My dolly has the flu.
Boo-hoo, hoo-hoo, hoo-hoo!
I've got no rainbow,
I've got no cellar door,
But we'll be jolly friends
Forevermore, more, more.

4

27

Arabba Gah Zee, Marissa and Me!

by Ruth Rosner

When I ask Marissa to play after school, she asks her mom. If the answer is yes, and it almost always is, Marissa calls, "Laura, RUN! We're being followed by spies!"

We race down the steep path past the school. Our mothers take the sidewalk.

When they meet up with us and ask, "How was school?" or "What did you have for lunch?" we pretend we don't understand English. Marissa says something like, "Arabba gah zee," which is supposed to mean "Quick! Up the wall!" I say, "Owamba la bah," which means "Wait for me!"

28

From the top of the wall, we can see my building. Whoever spots it first shouts, "Head for the hideout!"

Marissa protects me from the robots out front. I yell "SAFE!" when I touch the door.

You have to say the secret word if you want to get into the elevator.
Marissa's is "caterpillars" and mine is "swordfish." Then you push
the button three times and wait for the door to open.

If the spies follow us in, we disguise ourselves. Usually we're
famous ballerinas from the Royal Ballet at Covent Garden. We do
arabesques and grand pliés until the elevator gets to my floor.

Then we leap out the door to safety. Sometimes Marissa gets the
key and sometimes I do. We sneak it away while the spies are busy
talking.

Inside the hideout, we eat. We're soooooo hungry. We like green apples and green grapes better than tangerines. Marissa says cookies with filling give secret powers. I say the plain ones can turn you into monsters. We only take drinks that fizz.

As soon as we're done, we change into show clothes. Marissa's favorite colors are purple and pink. Mine are pink and red.

We pretend we're French gymnasts who do exercise to music. I'm ZSA ZSA. Marissa is GIGI. The audience sits on the couch—unless we get them to join us.

If we change into rock stars, Marissa wears the red boa. I get the feathers. We always serve hors d'oeuvres after the show.

If we don't know what to play next, we try on clothes until we get an idea—like playing sisters who are teenagers.

I'm Sherry and I usually break my arm and wear a cast. Marissa is Shelley and she breaks her leg and needs crutches. Sometimes we fight over the crutches. We always fight over the wheelchair.

Once when that happened, I got so mad I left the room and turned on the television. Another time, Marissa took a book into the bathroom and slammed the door.

Today when we started to fight, Marissa said, "Let's be pirates instead." "Great!" I said. "We can duel." I was just leaping over the ocean from my boat to Marissa's when our mothers walked in. "NO WATER IN THE LIVING ROOM!" they shouted.

So we quit that game, and I said, "Let's be sisters who are twins who get carried away by monsters who trap us in a cave."

The only way we could escape was to hide under blankets and sneak away into the night. It was a little too dark with the lights off and the shades down, so we had to use flashlights and bicycle reflectors.

Then we ran home to our baby sisters, who desperately needed baths and shampoos.

We left them to dry and made a potion powerful enough to turn us invisible. We mixed shampoos and soaps and toothpastes and powder and food coloring that turned the potion a perfect purple. We had just added the baking powder to make the whole thing bubble, when we heard, "LAURA! MARISSA! TIME TO CLEAN UP!"

It was awful! We had just started playing. We begged for one more minute.

"AT THE COUNT OF TEN!" said our mothers. And they began to count, just as they always do: "ONE... TWO... THREE... FOUR..."

Marissa and I did what *we* always do. We hid. But it was no use. We had to clean up. We threw all the play clothes into the basket and looked for Marissa's sneakers.

Then we had to say good-bye. I thanked Marissa for coming. And Marissa thanked me for the nice time. She promised we could finish our game soon at her house.

After Marissa left, I asked my mom if she wanted to play ballerinas.

She was pretty good. But no one's as good at playing as Marissa. Marissa says the same thing about me.

GROUP GAMES

These games are great for birthday parties, neighborhood gatherings, or family occasions—any time when there are lots of kids around, ready to play!

DUCK, DUCK, GOOSE!

Choose one person to be It. Everyone else sits in a circle. The person who is It walks around the circle, patting each player on the head as he passes. Each time he pats a head he says "Duck," until finally he decides to say "Goose!" The person whose head he patted when he said "Goose" jumps up and chases It around the circle. It runs around the circle until he comes to the goose's empty seat. If It can sit down before the goose touches him, he stays in the goose's place and the goose becomes It. But if the goose catches It, the original It must be It again.

NAME AND ROLL

Everyone sits in a circle. Two of the players have rubber balls. Each child with a ball calls out the name of another player in the circle and tries to roll the ball to her. Whoever catches the ball is the next to "name and roll." The fun comes when the balls collide as they roll across the circle.

RED LIGHT, GREEN LIGHT

Choose one person to be It. All the other players stand across the yard from It. It turns away, hides her eyes, and says, "Red light, green light, one, two, three!" While Its back is turned, the other players run toward her. On three, It turns around to face them, and they must freeze. As this is repeated, they move closer and closer to It, until finally one player is close enough to tag her. Whoever tags It first gets to be the next It.

MOTORBOAT, MOTORBOAT

Motorboat, motorboat,
Go so slow.
Motorboat, motorboat,
Go so fast.
Motorboat, motorboat,
Step on the gas!

Play this game outdoors on grass. Everyone stands in a circle, holding hands. The whole group starts moving around in a circle in one direction. Start out slowly, saying, "Motorboat, motorboat, go so slow." Then go around faster, saying, "Motorboat, motorboat, go so fast." Then everyone goes as fast as he can, singing, "Motorboat, motorboat, step on the gas!" Soon everyone is going so fast the circle comes apart!

COME FOLLOW ME!

Come follow me
And do what I do!

Shake your head side to side.
Now shake your hands, too.

Take one step out
And one step in.

Now turn like a top
Going spin, spin, spin!

Put your hands on the ground.
Now reach to the sky!

Spread your arms to the side
Like a plane zooming high.

Hop on one leg,
hop, hop, hop.

Now jump on two feet,
Jump, jump, stop.

Stand up tall.
Curl up in a ball.

Now hide your eyes
So you can't see at all!

This game is played like "Simon Says."
Just do the movements described,
by yourself or with friends.

WHERE IS EVERYBODY?

This is the Boyd family—Mr. Boyd, Mrs. Boyd, Jerry, and Lucy. Can you find them on this page and the pages that follow? Here's a hint: They always stay together in the crowd!

What a lovely day at the zoo!
Can you find the Boyds?

Can you also find:
one gorilla
five people wearing
   sunglasses
three blue balloons
four pink flamingos
the snake house
two arrows
one green picnic table
a toucan
a giant hot dog
one cowboy hat
three seals
two tigers
one giraffe

39

The Boyds are spending the day at the beach.
Can you find them?

See if you can also find:
two black inner tubes
four pink ice-cream cones
one blue Frisbee
one dragon-shaped kite
the blue-and-yellow-striped
  umbrella
a frisky puppy
a shivering swimmer
a sandcastle
a green baseball cap
two orange inflatable rafts
a bicycle built for two
a starfish
a camera

41

What a fantastic amusement park! Are the Boyds here today?

Also, where are:

two purple benches
one green boat
the number 7
a green-and-yellow bumper car
the red ticket stand
three red candy apples
one clown on stilts
a ringtoss game
four girls in blue overalls
three yellow balls
the camel on the merry-go-round
a mermaid

Play Ball!

When Everybody

When everybody bursts outdoors
Because they can't stay in,
Then oil your skates and count your jacks
And get a top to spin.

Then find your last year's skipping rope,
Then tape your baseball bat;
Then have a circus, charge a pin,
And be an acrobat.

Dorothy Aldis

45

Sycamore Soccer

by H.L. Ross

"*H*ooray!"

The Sycamore Stompers jumped up and down, cheering, as Jeannie Morrison kicked the black and white soccer ball past the goalie and into the net, winning the game. Cheering loudest of all was Emily Morrison. Her big sister, Jeannie, was the Stompers' star player. Emily was so proud of her. She couldn't wait to grow bigger, because she wanted to play on a soccer team, too.

As the players headed off the field, Emily ran out to the ball. By watching the big kids play, she had learned how to dribble the ball with the inside of her foot, how to kick with the top of her foot, and how to stop the ball with the bottom of her foot. Most important, she knew not to touch the ball with her hands. Only the goalie—the person who stood in front of the net—could use her hands.

"You're getting better all the time!" said Jeannie as she ran over to her little sister. Emily kicked the ball to Jeannie. As they often did after a game, the two sisters passed the ball back and forth as they ran up and down the field.

"But I'm still too small to play!" said Emily. "I'll never be big enough!"

"Sure you will!" Jeannie said. "Besides, size isn't that important in soccer. You've got to be fast and know how to handle the ball."

The next afternoon was practice. The Stompers divided themselves into two teams. They were short one player because Anne Evans was sick with the flu.

47

"Emily, do you want to play?" Jeannie asked.

Emily really wanted to join the game. But she was afraid she'd make a mistake, because she was still so small.

"C'mon, Emily!" said Jeannie. "Don't worry about how big you are. Just play the best you can, and have fun!"

At first, Emily played well. It was exciting! The other kids ran fast, and kicked far, but Emily was able to keep up. She was out of breath before long, but she was having a great time.

Emily kept on running, following the ball from one end of the field to the other. All of a sudden, Jeannie passed the ball to her. As Emily ran to kick it, she slipped in a big mud puddle and went sliding. Mud splashed into her face and covered her arms and legs.

"Are you all right?" asked Jeannie as she pulled Emily out of the puddle.

"Yeah, I'm okay," said Emily. "I guess I'm just too small to play on a team."

"Don't be silly," said Jeannie as she gave her sister a hug. "We all trip sometimes. It doesn't matter how big you are. All that matters is trying your best and having fun."

On the way home, Jeannie said, "We're playing a game against the Krazy Kickers tomorrow. Since Anne is sick, we're going to need another player. Why don't you play with us? I'm sure you can borrow Anne's uniform."

"I don't know," said Emily. "Do you think I'll grow much tonight?"

Jeannie and Emily both laughed. "I don't know," said Jeannie, "but if you are as quick tomorrow as you were today, you won't need to grow at all!"

The next day, Emily decided the only way to get better was to practice. She went into the backyard and began to kick her soccer ball around. She dribbled it down the yard as quickly as she could, then side-kicked it hard, straight through an opening in the fence.

"Good shot!" Emily said to herself, then ran to find the ball. She squeezed through the fence and started looking for it in the neighbor's bushes.

A few minutes later, Emily heard someone bouncing the ball. Looking up, she saw Lisa, the little girl next door. Lisa was even smaller than Emily. She was trying to *throw* the ball through a basketball hoop!

"Hey, Lisa!" Emily called over to her. "You kick it. You don't *throw* it! Come over and I'll show you."

So Emily showed Lisa how to dribble the soccer ball, how to pass it, and how to kick for a goal.

"This is fun!" laughed Lisa.

"Maybe you'll be a famous soccer player, someday," Emily said.

Lisa grinned. "I can't wait. I'm going to play soccer on a real team as soon as I'm a big kid—just like you!"

Emily couldn't believe her ears. "Me! A big kid!" she thought.

Just then, Jeannie came out of the house. "It's almost time for the game," she told Emily. "I've got a uniform for you. Let's go!"

Lisa handed Emily the soccer ball. "Can I come and watch?" she asked eagerly.

"Sure!" said Emily. "This will be fun!"

And the three of them went inside to get ready.

FIELD DAY

What do you do on field day? All kinds of races, games, and relays! Take a look at this field day and see what's happening! You can set up a field day in your own backyard with the games shown here or any others you know.

I'll get them this time!

Here's a stack of cereal boxes just waiting to be knocked down! Be sure to hit them just right with the ball—don't leave any boxes standing!

He did it on his third try.

Have you ever tried to race
with a cotton ball on a spoon?
If it falls off, just
pick it up and keep going.

Isn't it a lovely day for games?

Hurry! Hurry!

Get ready! Here I come!

Here's the relay race. You
hold the rolled-paper baton
and carry it to your teammate
as fast as you can! Then she
carries it to the next teammate.

Kick, Pass, and Run

by Leonard Kessler

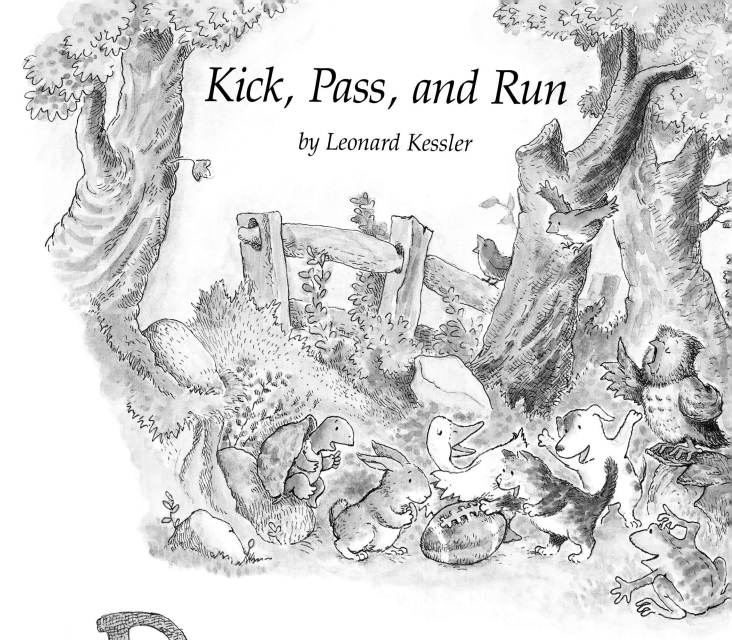

Rabbit was the first one to *hear* it. Duck was the first one to *see* it. Cat was the first one to *feel* it.

"What is it?" asked Dog. Owl said, "It's an egg!"

"An egg?" asked Frog. "Yes, an egg," said Owl. "It's an elephant's egg!" "No," said Turtle. "An elephant's egg is not brown."

Owl said, "It is a brown bear's egg."

"Bears do not lay eggs," said Duck. She laughed. "I can tell an egg when I see one. And that is *not* an egg!"

"Shhh," said Cat. "Someone is coming!" They all hid.

"Here it is," said a boy. "Here is our FOOTBALL!"

"It's a football," said Owl. "What is a football?" asked Frog.

"A football is a football," said Owl. "Let's go and see what the boys do with it," said Dog. They went up the hill.

They all hid. "Shhh. Be quiet," said Owl. "Let's see how boys play football."

They saw two teams on the football field. One team was the Jets. One team was the Giants.

"I am for the Jets," said Duck. "I am for the Giants," said Rabbit. "I am for *quiet*!" said Owl.

"Ready for the kickoff," yelled the Giants' kicker. He kicked the football. Up it went in the air.

The Jets' fullback caught the football. He ran up the field.

"Stop him! Tackle him!" yelled the Giants. "Wow," said Duck, "that looks like fun." She tackled Rabbit. "Stop that," said Cat.

The Jets went into a huddle. "The halfback will carry the ball around left end," said the quarterback.

Out of the huddle came the Jets. "First down and ten yards to go," said the Jets' quarterback. "Ready . . . Set . . . Down . . . Hup 1 . . . Hup 2 . . . Hup 3." The center gave him the ball.

"Hup 1 . . . Hup 2 . . . Hup 3. Hup 1 . . . Hup 2 . . . Hup 3," quacked Duck. "Oh, stop that," said Owl.

The quarterback flipped the football to the halfback. The halfback ran five yards before the Giants tackled him. "Go, team, go!" quacked Duck.

Out of the huddle came the Jets again. "Second down and five yards to go," said the quarterback. "Ready . . . Set . . . Down . . . Hup 1 . . . Hup 2 . . . Hup 3." He took the ball.

Back he went. Back. Back. "Look out for a forward pass," yelled the Giants. "Look out for a forward pass!" yelled Frog.

Up in the air went the football. Down it came to the Jets' halfback.

He caught the ball and ran and ran and ran all the way into the end zone.

"It's a TOUCHDOWN! A TOUCHDOWN! Six points for our team," yelled the Jets. "It's a touchdown," yelled Turtle.

"Wow," said Duck. "He made a touchdown." "What's a touchdown?" asked Frog. "A touchdown is six points," said Owl. "Let's play football," said Cat. "Yes," said Duck. "I want to make a touchdown."

Away they ran—back into the woods. "Here is a good spot to play," said Turtle. "Let's choose teams," said Owl. "Dog, Cat, Rabbit, Turtle, and Frog will be the Giants. And my team will be the Jets— Duck, the three little birds, and I!"

"That Owl," said Turtle, "is such a big boss." "Oh, forget it," said Dog. "Let's play football."

"But we need a football," said Frog. "How about an apple?" said Owl. "No, thanks," said Frog. "I'm not hungry."

"How about an apple for a football?" said Owl. "An apple will be fine," said Duck. "Let's play football!"

"Kickoff," said Owl. Up went the apple. Rabbit caught it and ran. He ran fast. Duck tackled him.

The Giants went into a huddle. "Frog will carry the ball around left end," Dog said softly.

Out of the huddle came the Giants. "First down and ten yards to go," said Dog. "Ready... Set... Down... Hup 1... Hup 2... Hup 3."

He got the apple. He gave it to Cat, who gave it to Rabbit, who gave it to Frog. All the Jets jumped on Frog.

"Who has the apple?" asked Owl. "Not me," said Rabbit. "Not me," said Cat. "Not me," said Dog. "No. Not me," said Turtle. They all looked at Frog.

"I guess I was hungry," said Frog. "You ATE THE FOOTBALL?" said Duck. "Now we need a new football."

"How about this paper bag?" asked Owl. "We can blow it up. That will make a good football."

Puff. Puff. Puff. He blew up the bag. "Some football," said Duck.

"It's our turn to get the ball," said Owl. "Ready . . . Set . . . Down . . ." "Hop 1 . . . Hop 2," quacked Duck. "Not Hop," said Owl. "It's Hup." "Up?" said Duck.

She took the ball and up in the air she flew. "No fair! No fair!" yelled Rabbit. "You can't fly! Only the ball can go in the air."

"Yes, I can," said Duck. "No, you can't." "Yes, I can, you stupid Rabbit." "No, you can't, you silly Duck." "Oh, oh. Another fight," said Frog.

"Stop it! Stop it!" said Owl. "That's not the way to play football." "Then I won't play," said Duck.

"Oh, let her go," said Turtle. "But we *need* her," said Dog. "The teams won't be even."

"Come back and play. We need you," said Owl. "Okay," said Duck. She picked up the paper-bag football. "Time for a big kickoff," said Duck.

"YOU CAN'T KICK THE PAPER BAG!" shouted Owl.

But it was too late. Up went the bag. POP!

"No more football," said Dog. "That's the end of the game," said Turtle.

Whissh! Rabbit was the first one to *hear* it. Duck was the first one to *see* it. And Cat was the first one to *catch* it! "It's a REAL FOOTBALL!" he shouted.

And away he went. "Tackle him!" yelled Owl. "Stop him! Stop him!" quacked Duck.

But they did not catch him. He ran and ran and ran.

"Touchdown!" "Touchdown!" "Six points for the Giants!" Rabbit hopped up and down.

"Look out! Someone is coming," shouted Frog. Cat dropped the football. They all hid.

"Here it is," said the boy. "Here is our football. I wonder how it got way back here?"

Little People™ Big Book About PLAYTIME

TIME-LIFE for CHILDREN™

Publisher: Robert H. Smith
Managing Editor: Neil Kagan
Editorial Directors: Jean Burke Crawford,
　　　　　Patricia Daniels
Editorial Coordinator: Elizabeth Ward
Marketing Director: Ruth P. Stevens
Product Manager: Margaret Mooney
Production Manager: Prudence G. Harris
Administrative Assistant: Rebecca C. Christoffersen
Editorial Consultants: Jacqueline A. Ball, Sara Mark

PRODUCED BY PARACHUTE PRESS, INC.

Editorial Director: Joan Waricha
Editors: Christopher Medina, Jane Stine, Wendy Wax
Writers: H.L. Ross, Natalie Standiford, Jean Waricha,
　　　　　Wendy Wax
Designer: Deborah Michel
Illustrators: Robert Alley (p.58-63), Shirley Beckes
　　　　　(endpapers, title page), Paige Billings-Frye
　　　　　(p. 12-17), Maryann Cocca-Leffler (p. 26-
　　　　　27, 46-51), Paul Harvey (p. 38-43), Ann
　　　　　Iosa (p. 18-23), Barbara Lonza (p. 6-11),
　　　　　Ruth Rosner (p. 28-33), John Speirs (cover,
　　　　　p. 4-5, 24-25, 34-37, 44-45, 52-57).

Time-Life Books Inc. is a wholly owned subsidiary
of THE TIME INC. BOOK COMPANY.

TIME-LIFE is a trademark of Time Warner Inc. U.S.A.

FISHER-PRICE, LITTLE PEOPLE and AWNING
DESIGN are trademarks of Fisher-Price, Division of
The Quaker Oats Company, and are used under
license.

Time-Life Books Inc. offers a wide range of fine
publications, including home video products. For
subscription information, call 1-800-621-7026, or
write TIME-LIFE BOOKS, P.O. Box C-32068, Rich-
mond, Virginia 23261-2068.

ACKNOWLEDGMENTS

Every effort has been made to trace the ownership of all copyrighted material and to secure the necessary
permissions to reprint these selections. If any question arises as to the use of any material, the editor and the
publisher, while expressing regret for any inadvertent error, will make the necessary correction in future
printings.

Grateful acknowledgment is made to the following for permission to reprint copyrighted material: Curtis
Brown Ltd. for "We're Racing, Racing down the Walk" from THE ABC OF BEING A GIRL by Phyllis Mc-
Ginley. Copyright © 1959, 1960 by Phyllis McGinley. Renewed © 1987 by Mrs. Richard Blake, 1988 by Patricia
Blake. HarperCollins Publishers for KICK, PASS, AND RUN by Leonard Kessler. Copyright © 1966 by Leon-
ard Kessler. GP Putnam's Sons for "When Everybody" from BEFORE THINGS HAPPEN by Dorothy Aldis.
Copyright © 1930 by Dorothy Aldis. Renewed © 1967 by Mary Cornelia Aldis Porter. Albert Whitman & Co.
for ARABBA GAH ZEE, MARISSA AND ME! by Ruth Rosner. Text copyright © 1987 by Ruth Rosner.

Library of Congress Cataloging-in-Publication Data

Little people big book about playtime.
　　p.　cm.
　　Summary: A collection of stories, poems, and songs about play and games. Also includes games
and activities.
　　ISBN 0-8094-7516-2—ISBN 0-8094-7517-0 (lib. bdg.)
　　　1. Play—Literary collections. 2. Games—Literary collections. [1. Play—Literary collections.
2. Games—Literary collections. 3. Games.] I. Time-Life for Children (Firm)
PZ5.LZ2583　1990
810.8'0355—dc20
　　　　　　　　　　　　　　　　　　　　　　　　　　90-42795
　　　　　　　　　　　　　　　　　　　　　　　　　　CIP
　　　　　　　　　　　　　　　　　　　　　　　　　　AC

TIME-LIFE BOOKS
ALEXANDRIA, VIRGINIA

Playtime

Twist around,
Turn around,
Twirl around, and then
Swish about
And spin about,
And do it all again!

Twist around,
Whirl around,
As you have done before;
Spin about
And turn about,
And do it all once more!

Watch the spins,
Watch the turns,
Watch the twists and twirls,
In and out
And roundabout,
For busy boys and girls.

Unknown